Dear Family and Friends of New Readers,

Welcome to Scholastic Reader. We have taken more than eighty years' experience with teachers, parents, and children and put it into a program that is designed to match your child's interest and skills. Each Scholastic Reader is designed to support your child's efforts to learn how to read at every age and every stage.

- First Reader
- Preschool - Kindergarten
- ABC's
- First words

- Beginning Reader
- Preschool - Grade 1
- Sight words
- Words to sound out
- Simple sentences

- Developing Reader
- Grades 1 – 2
- New vocabulary
- Longer sentences

- Growing Reader
- Grades 1 – 3
- Reading for inspiration and information

On the back of every book, we have indicated the grade level, guided reading level, Lexile® level, and word count. You can use this information to find a book that is a good fit for your child.

For ideas about sharing books with your new reader, please visit www.scholastic.com. Enjoy helping your child learn to read and love to read!

Happy Reading!

—**Francie Alexander**
Chief Academic Officer
Scholastic Inc.

*For Melia and Mimi with love,
and with thanks to Dave and Dan
—J.M.*

*For Betty Wick
—W.W.*

Text copyright © 2009 by Jean Marzollo.
Illustrations and photographs compilation copyright © 2009 by Walter Wick from *I Spy: A Book of Picture Riddles* © 1992, *I Spy Mystery* copyright © 1993 by Walter Wick, *I Spy School Days* copyright © 1995 by Walter Wick, *I Spy Spooky Night* copyright © 1998 by Walter Wick. All published by Scholastic Inc.

Library of Congress Cataloging-in-Publication Data.

Marzollo, Jean.

I spy I love you / by Jean Marzollo ; illustrated by Walter Wick.

p. cm. -- (Scholastic reader. Level 1)

ISBN 978-0-545-12513-0

1. Picture puzzles--Juvenile literature. 2. Love--Juvenile literature. I. Wick, Walter, ill. II. Title. III. Series.

GV1507.P47M293 2009

793.73--dc22

2009030022

ISBN 978-0-545-24179-3

10 9   11 12 13/0

Printed in the U.S.A. 40 • First printing, December 2009

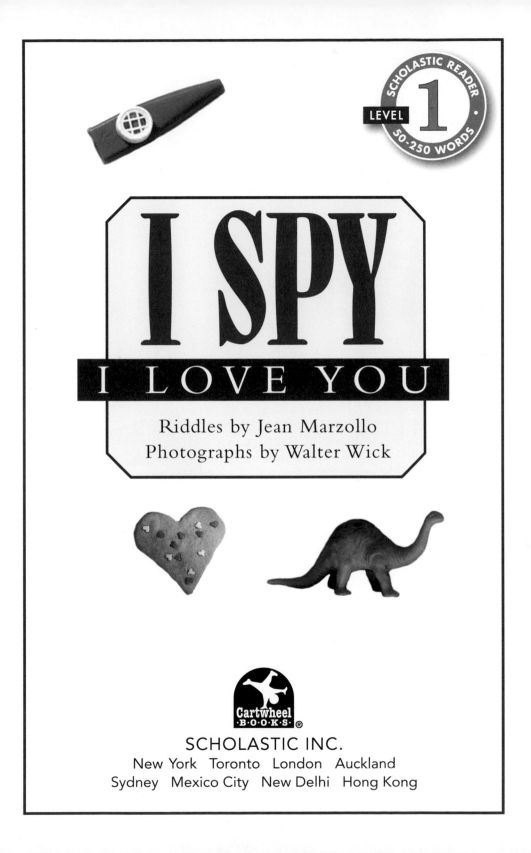

SCHOLASTIC READER
LEVEL 1
50-250 WORDS

I SPY
I LOVE YOU

Riddles by Jean Marzollo
Photographs by Walter Wick

Cartwheel
·B·O·O·K·S·®
SCHOLASTIC INC.
New York   Toronto   London   Auckland
Sydney   Mexico City   New Delhi   Hong Kong

I spy

a heart,

 a yellow hat,

a fish,

ONE MUST
NOT TIE
A SHIP
TO A
SINGLE
ANCHORS
NOR LIFE
TO A
SINGLE
HOPE.
EPICTETVS E

HOPE,

and a huggable cat.

I spy

a metal jet,

 a cart,

a dinosaur,

 and an upside-down heart.

I spy

a spring,

a little guitar,

a bride,

a groom,

and a red race car.

I spy

 a bridge,

a door in a tree,

 a red lantern,

and MOM & ME.

I spy

a ladder,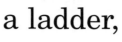

a kangaroo,

BE MINE,

a crown,

and a blue kazoo.

I spy

a comb,

a shoe on a bed,

a doll to love,

and a bow that's red.

I spy

a couple,

 a deer,

a horse,

and Be My Valentine, of course.

I spy

 a family,

the number 2,

 home plate,

and I will marry you.

I spy

a shovel,

a broom that's small,

a wooden heart,

and a wooden ball.

I spy

 a dolphin,

a sail that's blue,

 an orange crayon,

and I LOVE YOU.

I spy two matching words.

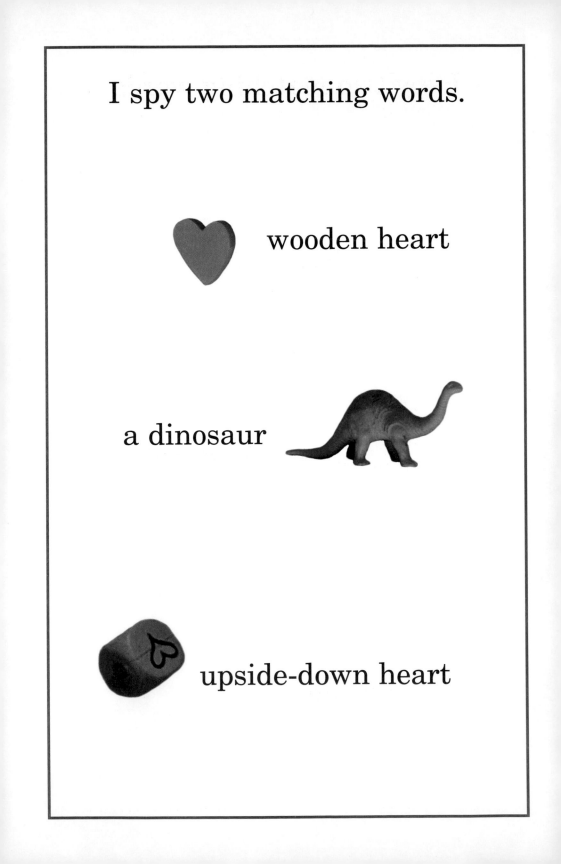

wooden heart

a dinosaur

upside-down heart

I spy two matching words.

BE MINE

Be My Valentine

a bride

I spy two words that start with the letter H.

a groom

 home plate

HOPE

I spy two words that start with the letters BR.

bridge

bride

a kangaroo

I spy two words that end
with the letter R.

ladder

dinosaur

a blue kazoo

I spy two words that end
with the letters LE.

 couple

a doll to love

 huggable cat

I spy two words that rhyme.

groom

a deer

broom that's small

I spy three words that rhyme.

shoe on a bed

blue kazoo

a horse